MEETINGS:

To Do:

Special Dates:

SEPTEMBER
Classroom Themes:

Books To Check Out:

Materials To Collect:

Duties This Month:

Birthdays:

©1999 The Education Center, Inc. • September Monthly Reproducibles • Kindergarten • TEC955

SEPTEMBER

Miller

From Your Friends At **The MAILBOX®**

SEPTEMBER

A MONTH OF REPRODUCIBLES AT YOUR FINGERTIPS!

Kindergarten

Editor:
Angie Kutzer

Contributing Editors:
Jayne M. Gammons, Ada Goren, Mackie Rhodes

Writers:
Joe Appleton, Marilee Burton, Rhonda L. Dominguez, Diane Gilliam,
Lucia Kemp Henry, Kathleen K. Padilla, Kelli Plaxco

Art Coordinator:
Clevell Harris

Artists:
Jennifer Tipton Bennett, Cathy Spangler Bruce, Pam Crane,
Teresa Davidson, Clevell Harris, Lucia Kemp Henry, Sheila Krill,
Kimberly Richard, Rebecca Saunders, Donna K. Teal

Cover Artist:
Jennifer Tipton Bennett

©1999 by THE EDUCATION CENTER, INC.
All rights reserved.
ISBN #1-56234-272-X

Manufactured in the United States
10 9 8 7 6 5 4 3 2 1

Table Of Contents

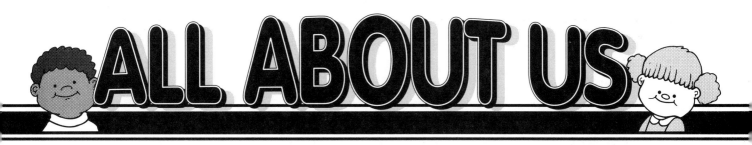

ALL ABOUT US

Promote self-awareness and self-esteem in your kindergartners with these fun ideas.

Same Or Different?

Here's an activity to help your youngsters develop an appreciation for their similarities and differences. In advance, duplicate a class supply of page 6; then read *We Are All Alike… We Are All Different* by the Cheltenham Elementary School Kindergartners (Scholastic Inc.). Discuss the similarities and differences of the children in the book. Then invite youngsters to discuss some of the similarities and differences found among themselves, such as hair color, height, and shoe size. Have each child illustrate a class-mate for each box on page 6; then write his dictation on the lines. During group time, invite each child to tell the class about his illustrations. It's great to be alike…and different!

I Am…

Build self-awareness in youngsters with this guessing game. To prepare, write each child's name on a separate notecard; then place the cards in a paper bag. Explain to students that you will draw a card from the bag. Then, without telling the name of the child, you will describe that child as if you were him. For example, you might say, "I am a boy with brown eyes and red hair." Encourage students to guess the described child, adding clues as necessary until the child is identified. Then invite the selected child to tell a few more things about himself.

Kindergarten "Me-ographies"

Students will create cherished keepsakes with these simple autobiographies. Duplicate pages 7 and 8 for each child. Working with one small group at a time, have each child cut apart her booklet pages. Then help her complete her booklet as suggested, writing her dictation on each page. Stack and staple the pages of each booklet together; then invite each youngster to read her autobiography to the group.

Cover: Draw a self-portrait; then write your name on the line.

Page 1: Illustrate your home.

Page 2: Draw hair on the head to resemble your hair.

Page 3: Color the eyes to match your eye color.

Page 4: Draw the number of candles on the cake to equal your age.

Page 5: Illustrate a food.

Page 6: Use your favorite color to color the crayon.

Page 7: Draw a picture from your favorite book.

My
Autobiography
A story about me!

By Lindsay

My favorite color is
red

Same

This is _____. We have the same

_____.

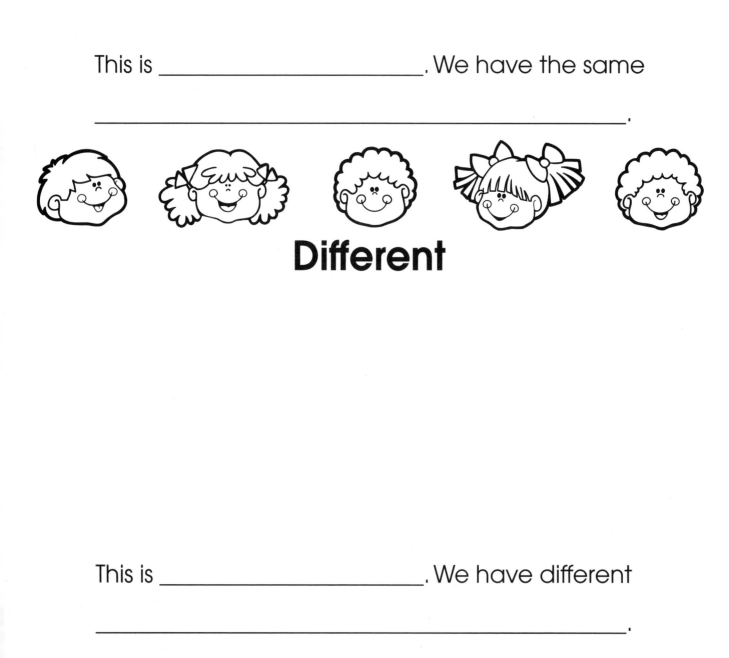

Different

This is _____. We have different

_____.

My
Autobiography
A Story About Me!

By _____

©1999 The Education Center, Inc.

I live

_____ .

1

My hair is

_____ .

2

My eyes are

_____ .

3

Booklet Pages
Use with "Kindergarten 'Me-ographies'" on page 5.

I am _____ years old.

4

I like to eat

_____ .

5

My favorite color is

_____ .

6

My favorite book is

_____ .

7

HAPPY BIRTHDAY!

Reinforce basic concepts by using common events well known to most kindergartners—birthdays. These activities will spark lively discussions as youngsters turn skills practice into a party!

Gotta Have Balloons!

A birthday just wouldn't be complete without balloons. Obtain a class supply of balloons and small slips of paper. On each piece of paper, write a different letter or numeral before inserting it into a balloon. Blow up the balloons and place them in a large trash bag. Have one student at a time get a balloon and bounce on it until it pops. Then instruct her to name the symbol on the enclosed paper and tell whether it's a letter or a numeral. (Encourage your children to help fellow classmates who can not yet recognize the symbols.) Follow up this "pop-ular" party game with the reproducibles on pages 11 and 12 for independent practice.

Birthday Bingo

Have a blast playing Birthday Bingo with your little ones. Duplicate a class supply of the bingo card on page 13 onto construction paper; then cut them out. Program the star on each card with a different child's name. Then use the pictures at the bottom of the pages to program the boxes on the cards so that each card is different. To create caller cards, label a separate notecard with the name of each of the pictures represented on the bingo cards.

To play, give each child her personalized bingo card and a supply of markers. Mix up the notecards and call them out one by one until a player scores bingo—three in a row. Invite the winner to tell everyone her birthdate and what she would like to do for her next birthday. Then clear the cards and play another round!

Summer Birthday Solution

A summer birthday can be a real party pooper. Give each youngster whose birthday is in a summer month a half-year birthday celebration! Simply add six months to each child's summer birthday; then celebrate her birthday on that day. Be sure to sing a lively round of "Happy Half-Birthday" to the special honoree.

When Were *You* Born?

January	▨▨▨								
February	▨▨▨								
March									
April	▨								
May	▨▨▨▨▨								
June	▨▨								
July									
August									
September	▨▨▨▨								
October	▨▨								
November	▨								
December	▨▨▨▨▨								

Shapes Take The Cake

Encouraging creativity, shape recognition, counting, and fine-motor skills is a piece of cake with this activity. Duplicate the cake on page 14 onto construction paper for each child. Cut or die-cut a supply of small colorful squares, triangles, rectangles, and circles from construction paper. Have the child color her cake, then use some of the shapes to decorate her cake in any way she chooses. Direct her to count and record on the designated lines the number of shapes used. As a finishing touch, have the child glue actual birthday-cake candles to her cake to represent her age on her next birthday. Keep the cakes to display on each child's birthday (or half-birthday).

Birthdays Galore!

Group youngsters by their birthdays with this class graph. In advance, create a large graph on chart paper to resemble the graph shown here. Call out the name of each month. Ask students with birthdays in that month to stand; then invite each child to color a block beside that month on the graph to indicate his birthday. After the class graph is completed, have youngsters compare the months with the most and fewest birthdays. Extend this idea by helping your children compile a graph of their family members' birthdays for comparison.

Cassie

How many △s? 4
How many ▭s? 4
How many □s? 3
How many Os? 4

10

A Birthday Bakery

Set up a special birthday bakery for your birthday unit or to celebrate each child's birthday. Supply a center with lots of colorful play dough, along with birthday candles, small cake pans, cookie cutters, rolling pins, and cupcake liners. Then invite youngsters to create their own imaginary birthday treats to celebrate their special days. Happy birthday to you!

Balloon Bouquets

Color.

Cut.

Glue each balloon to its correct bouquet.

11

Make A Wish

Help Birdie find his way to his birthday cake by coloring only the balloons labeled with numerals.

Bonus Box: What would you wish for if it was your birthday? Draw your wish on the back of this paper.

©1999 The Education Center, Inc. • *September Monthly Reproducibles* • Kindergarten • TEC955

Birthday Bingo

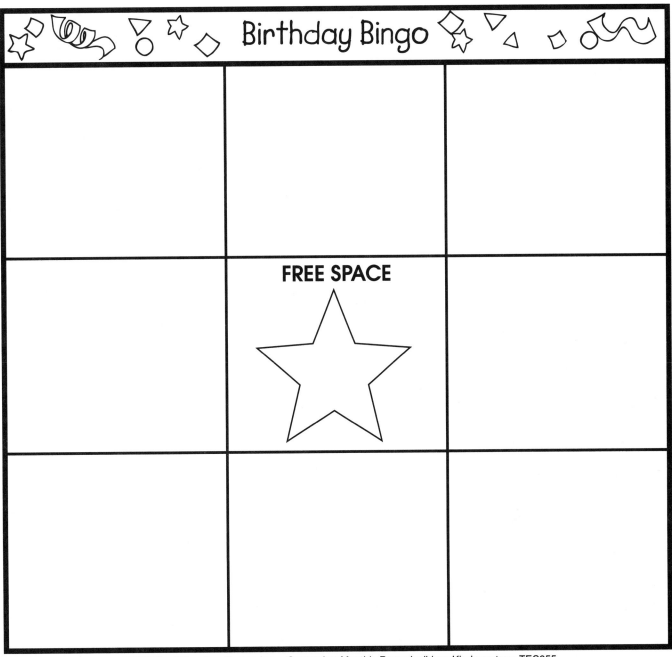

	FREE SPACE	

Happy Birthday!

Cake Pattern
Use with "Shapes Take The Cake" on page 10.

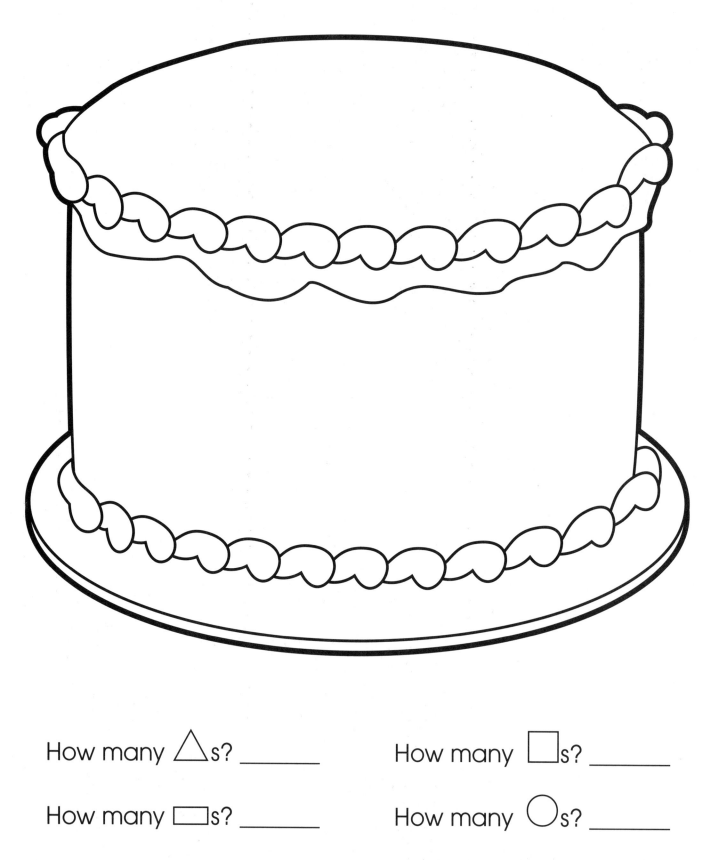

How many △s? _____   How many □s? _____

How many ▭s? _____   How many ○s? _____

LABOR DAY

Combine youngsters' knowledge about jobs and careers with the ideas in this hardworking unit to gain a better understanding of Labor Day.

"What Did You Do At Work Today?"

Do your youngsters know what their parents do at work? Encourage them to find out; then have them report their findings with this activity. Send a note home to parents asking them to tell their children about the work they do. Ask them to send in a work-related item—such as a piece of equipment, an article of clothing, or even a photograph—on a specific day. On the appointed day, invite each child to proudly display his parent's work item as he tells about his parent's important job. Be sure to have extra chairs on hand for this special event—someone just might bring his *parent* in for this special show-and-tell!

Tools Of The Trade

Reinforce student knowledge about the tools used for different jobs with the reproducible on page 16. Duplicate the page for each child. Then explain that the worker in each picture is missing a necessary tool. Ask students to complete the page as indicated; then discuss the different occupations represented on the page. For added fun, play a quick game of charades, starting with the pictured occupations.

When I Grow Up…

Help your little ones explore the "working world" as they make these career headbands. Provide each child with a sentence strip, scissors, glue, and access to a collection of magazines. Before beginning the activity, look through a magazine together and discuss a few illustrations that show people doing various kinds of work. Then have each youngster look through a magazine, cut out several pictures of working people, and glue them to her sentence strip. Staple the ends of the child's sentence strip together to fit her head; then invite her to tell about her favorite occupation that's represented on her headband.

Tools Of The Trade

 Color.   ✂ Cut.   Glue.

Bonus Box: On the back of your paper, draw a picture of what you want to do when you grow up. What tools will you use?

Hooray For Houses!

Youngsters will feel right at home with these curriculum-related reproducibles about houses.

It's Geometric!

Build student skills in shape and color recognition with this activity. Duplicate page 19 for each child. Explain that a house is made of many different shapes. For example, its door might be a rectangle, whereas its windows are square, and its roof is a triangle. Then have the class identify each shape represented on page 19. Guide your youngsters in filling in the color key with the appropriate colors; then direct them to complete the page using the key as a guide. If possible, extend this activity by taking a walk around the school's neighborhood to view some shapely houses.

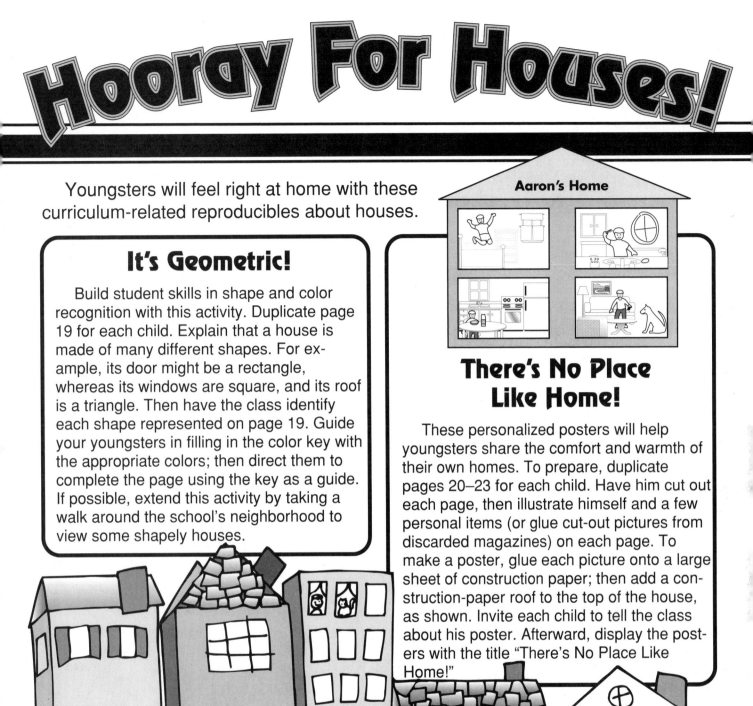

Aaron's Home

There's No Place Like Home!

These personalized posters will help youngsters share the comfort and warmth of their own homes. To prepare, duplicate pages 20–23 for each child. Have him cut out each page, then illustrate himself and a few personal items (or glue cut-out pictures from discarded magazines) on each page. To make a poster, glue each picture onto a large sheet of construction paper; then add a construction-paper roof to the top of the house, as shown. Invite each child to tell the class about his poster. Afterward, display the posters with the title "There's No Place Like Home!"

A Showcase Of Homes

Youngsters will be proud to show off their home-decorating savvy with this showcase of homes. In advance, collect an assortment of boxes in a variety of sizes and shapes. Invite each child to select a box to paint the color of her choice. After the paint dries, encourage her to add special features to the box, such as construction-paper windows and doors; a cardboard roof shingled with torn tissue paper; and pom-pom flowers. Have youngsters arrange their homes in a tabletop display complete with construction-paper streets and toy vehicles; then invite parents, school staff, and other classes to tour your showcase of homes. Beautiful!

Building From Blueprints

Introduce youngsters to a bit of building terminology with this activity. Explain to your class that an *architect* is a person who designs a house. He creates a *blueprint* of his design by drawing it with blue ink on large sheets of paper. The *builder* then builds a real house by following the instructions and design of the blueprint. Invite each child to the easel to create a blueprint of a house using a blue marker. Afterward, have him take his blueprint to the block center as a reference for building his dream house.

Here A House, There A House

Bring the surrounding neighborhood right into your classroom with this class mural. To prepare, have students paint a simple background of grass and sky on a length of white bulletin-board paper. Then invite each child to make an individual illustration of her house, apartment, trailer, etc. Help the child cut out her house and glue it to the mural. Label each child's home with her name. Once all of the dwellings are on the mural, paint on a street that connects the homes together. Encourage youngsters to finish the display by adding drawings of trees, flowers, and other unique items found in their neighborhood.

Heading Home

Do your students know their way home? Although they may not be able to name specific street names and directions, chances are they know landmarks along the way! During group time, invite each child to tell about some of the landmarks she might pass on her way home from school. Follow up this discussion by giving each child a copy of page 24. Have her complete the maze and color the pictures.

It's Geometric!

Color:

△ —brown   ▢ —red   ◯ —blue   ▭ —yellow

Poster Page
Use with "There's No Place Like Home!" on page 17.

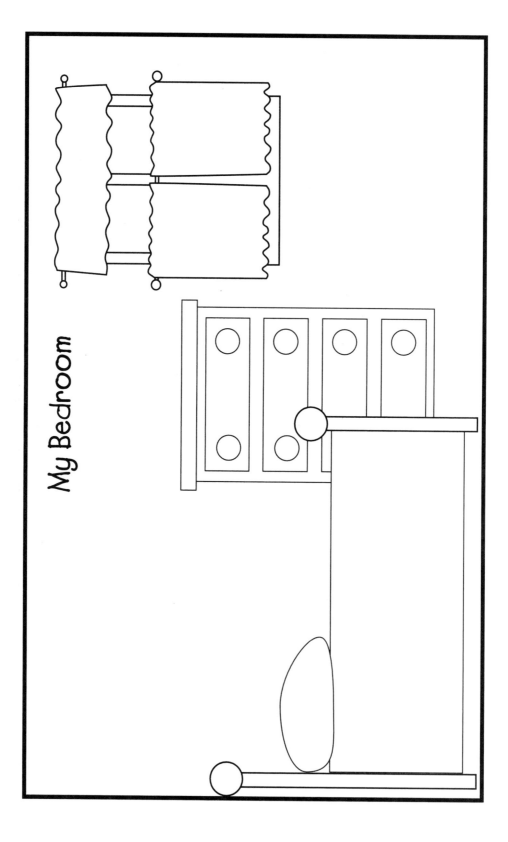

©1999 The Education Center, Inc. • *September Monthly Reproducibles* • Kindergarten • TEC955

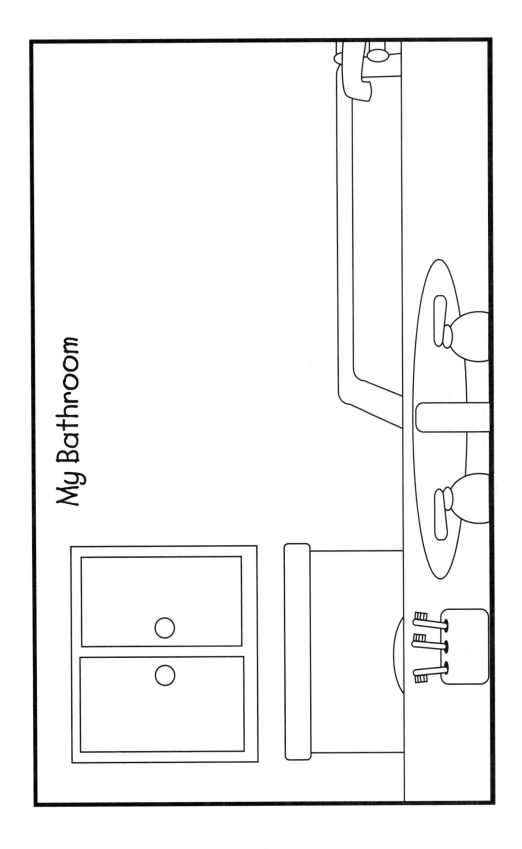

My Bathroom

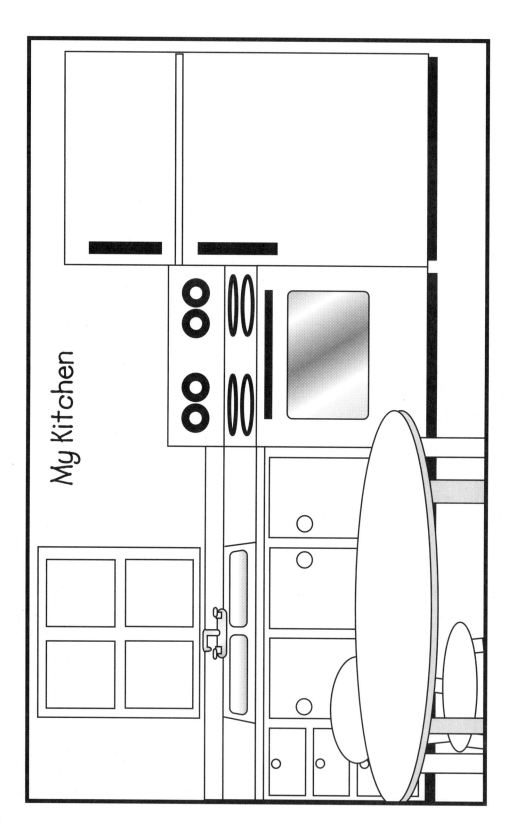

My Living Room

Name_____

Heading Home

Trace a path.

Color.

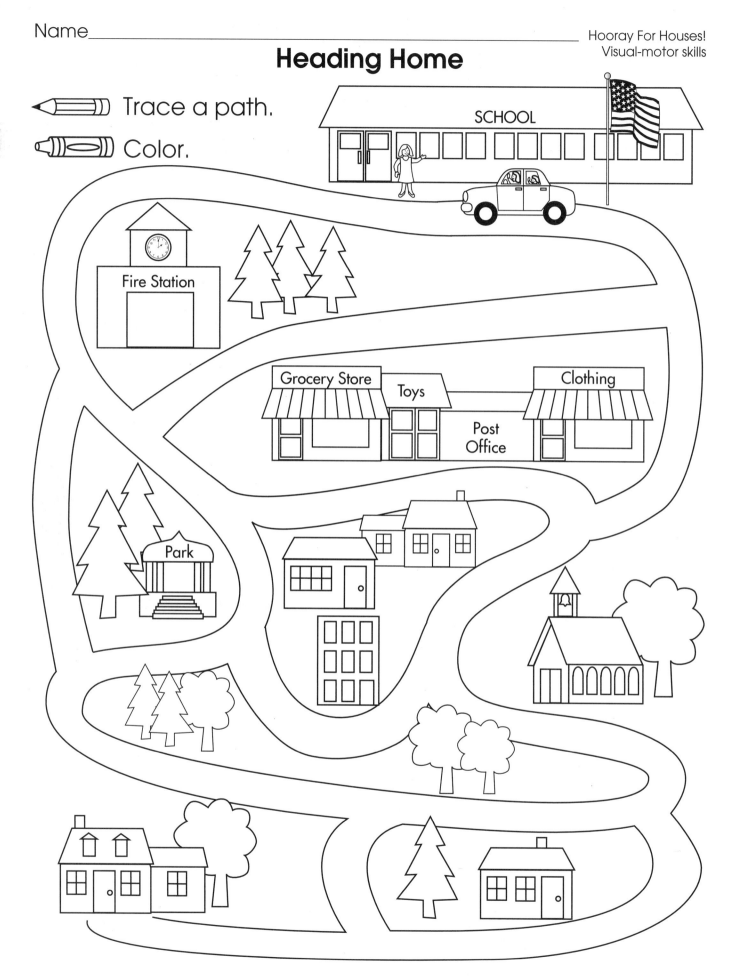

©1999 The Education Center, Inc. • *September Monthly Reproducibles* • Kindergarten • TEC955

GRANDPARENTS DAY

Here are two ideas that pay tribute to those tremendously special, *experienced* (not old!) people in your students' lives—grandparents!

Aren't They Grand?

Gather your little ones around some chart paper and discuss why grandparents are so grand. List each child's response; then leave room on the paper for the child to illustrate his statement. After all of the responses have been illustrated, post the tribute so that grandparents can read it when visiting the classroom.

Grover: My grandparents buy pizzas on Fridays!

A Special Report

These front-page features are guaranteed to make grandparents and senior friends puff up with pride! Explain to youngsters that they will assume the roles of reporters to interview their grandparents or senior friends. Then send home a copy of the parent note (this page) and page 26 with each child. When the child brings her form back to school, cut it out; glue it onto an 8" x 11" sheet of newspaper; then glue the newspaper to a 9" x 12" sheet of construction paper. After each child shares her report with the class, encourage her to deliver this special edition to her grandparent or friend in recognition of Grandparents Day.

The Grandparent Press

Vol. 1 No. 1   "All the news about special grandparents"   25 cents

Student Interviews
Interesting Grandparent

by ___Lucia___
(child's name)

My grandparent likes me!
My grandparent is _sweet and loving_

We like to _read and draw_ together.

Sometimes we play _crazy eights_

I like my grandparent because _she teaches me how to do lots of things_

Grandparent Briefs:
Name: _Mary Griffith_
Hobby: _Bird watching_
Favorite Food: _avocado_
Favorite Book: _The Secret Garden_

A Great Grandparent

Dear Parent,

Our class is writing newspaper reports as a salute to Grandparents Day. Please help your child interview a grandparent or senior friend, then record the information on *The Grandparent Press* form. Have your child complete the page by attaching a photo of the featured person or by drawing an illustration.

Please have your child return the report to school by

_____.

Thanks for your help!

Interview Form
Use with "A Special Report" on page 25.

The Grandparent Press

Vol. 1 No. 1   "All the news about special grandparents"   25 cents

Student Interviews Interesting Grandparent

by _____
(child's name)

My grandparent likes me!

My grandparent is _____

_____.

We like to _____

_____ together.

Sometimes we play _____

_____.

I like my grandparent because

_____

_____

_____.

Grandparent Briefs:

Name: _____

Hobby: _____

Favorite Food: _____

Favorite Book: _____

_____

A Great Grandparent

Forever Friends

Reinforce good-friend qualities with the activities in this child-friendly unit.

Friends At School

Here's an idea that will help youngsters focus on their friends at school. To begin, write a student-generated list of fun things your children do with their friends. Invite each child to think of a friend at school whom he likes to play with. Give him a copy of page 28 on which to illustrate himself and his friend engaged in an enjoyable school activity. Write his dictation to complete the sentence on the page. Then, during group time, encourage each child to share his picture with the class.

Sharing And Caring

Your classroom will be filled with sharing and caring friends when you present these fabulous friends awards. Duplicate and cut out a supply of the awards on page 29. Then duplicate the pattern on page 30 onto tagboard. Cut out the tagboard pattern; then attach it to a wide craft stick to create friendship spectacles. Once or twice during the day, find two or more students engaged in good-friend behaviors. Hold up the glasses and recite the verse below, naming the involved students and their activity. Afterward, present each child with a friendship award. What a neat way to encourage friendships at the beginning of the year!

Good friends, good friends,
Who do I spy today?
[Child's name] and [Child's name] are [name of activity].
Hip, hip, hooray!

The Buddy Basics

Practicing the basics can be fun—*if* you're practicing with a buddy. Pair up students and have them work together to complete a copy of pages 31 and 32. They'll learn cooperation and teamwork as well as patterning and counting.

My friends at school are really cool!

with _____.

I like to _____

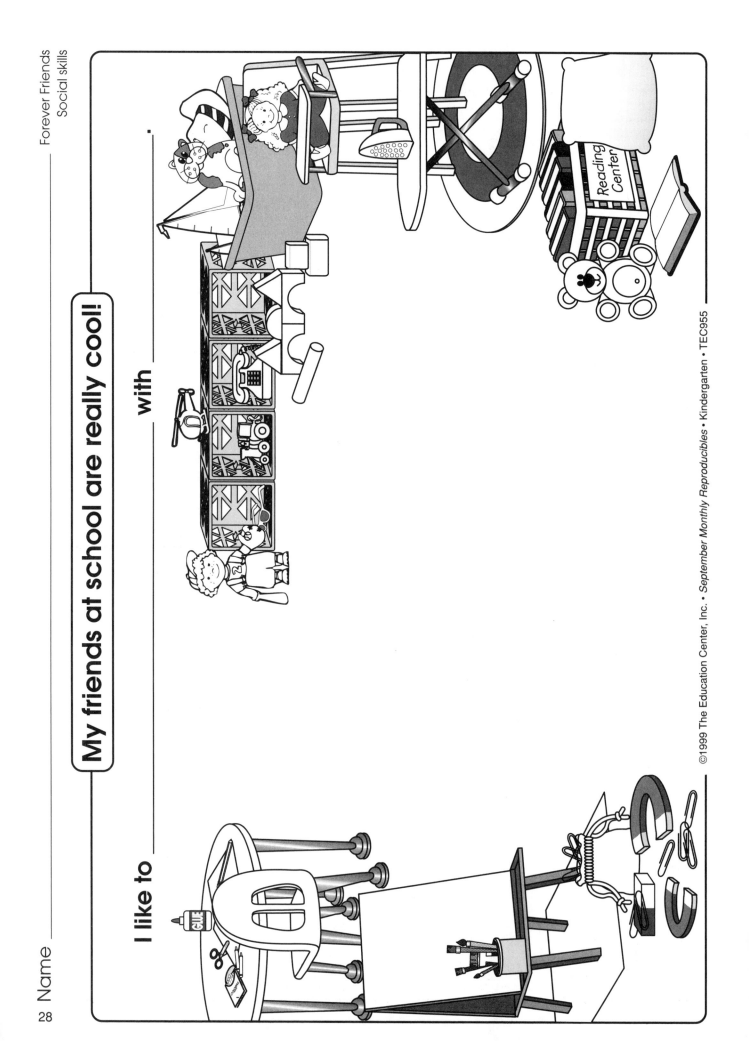

_____
(Name)

Was A Fabulous Friend Today!

_____
(Date)

This Sharing & Caring Award is presented to

_____
(Name)

_____
(Date)

Pattern
Use with "Sharing And Caring" on page 27.

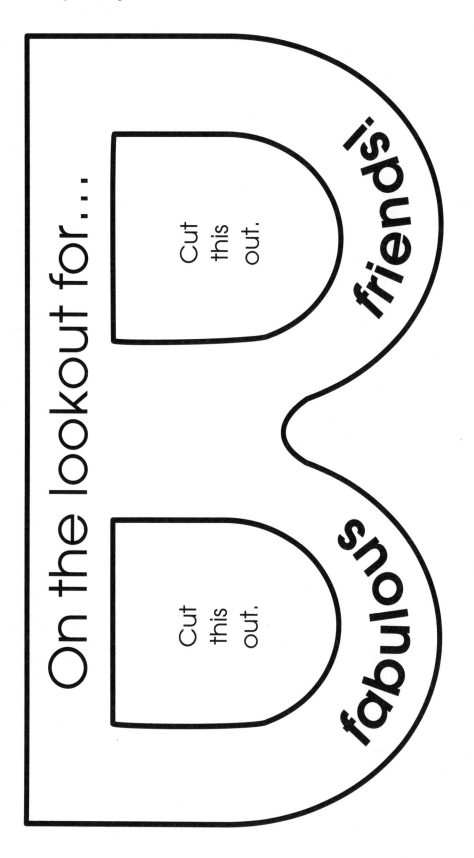

On the lookout for...

Cut this out.

Cut this out.

friends!

fabulous

Playground Fun

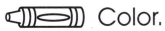 Circle the correct numeral.

 Color.

| 4 | 2 | | 5 | 2 |

| 3 | 4 | | 3 | 5 |

Pattern Pals

Cut.

Complete each pattern.

Glue.

32

Check out these ideas designed to motivate youngsters to sign up for library cards—*and* to make regular visits to their local library.

Sign On The Line

Use this sign-up board to capitalize on kindergartners' fascination with name writing. To prepare, program a poster with rows of lines as shown. Hang the poster in the reading center along with a pencil. Instruct youngsters to sign their names on the poster each time they visit the reading center to select a book. When the poster is filled with names, replace it with a new one.

Check It Out

Encourage youngsters to use pretend library cards to check out books in your classroom library. To begin, set up your reading center to resemble a library. To one side, arrange a checkout counter. Stock the counter with notecards, pencils, stamps, stamp pads, and a file box. Appoint a student to be the librarian. During center time, direct each visitor to sign up for a library card at the checkout counter (write his name on a notecard). Then have him circulate through the library to make a book selection. Afterward, direct him back to the counter to have his library card stamped and filed. Encourage your young library patrons to read and then return their books to the library. At the end of the week, ask each child to count and report to the class the number of stamps on his card.

I Went To The Library

Take your students to the local library so that they can see book-borrowing procedures in true-life fashion. During your tour, encourage youngsters to remember the many things that they see and learn. Back in the classroom, invite each child to illustrate a copy of page 34 with something she saw at the library. Then have her take her illustration home to share with family members. Hopefully, entire families will visit the library together and sign up for their own personal library cards!

I went to the library and what did I see?

Dear Parent,

   September is Library Card Sign-Up Month. To celebrate this occasion, we took a trip to our local library. Ask your child to tell you about the many things we saw and learned on our trip.

   Why not return to the library with your kindergartner—and your entire family—to have everyone sign up for a personal library card? You'll be glad you did!

 ©1999 The Education Center, Inc. • *September Monthly Reproducibles* • Kindergarten • TEC955

It's NURSERY RHYME TIME!

These fun-packed activities will give new rhythm to some of Mother Goose's traditional favorites.

Lift the crust to take a peek.
What do you see?
This is what I'd like to have
Baked in a pie for me!

My Pie

Sing a song of sixpence, a pocket full of rye. What would *you* like to see baked in a pie? Share the traditional rhyme with youngsters; then give each child a construction-paper copy of pages 37 and 38. To make a pie, a child colors the piecrust on page 38, then cuts out the patterns on each page. He then glues pieces of foil on the pie tin and a magazine cutout of a favorite food on the pie. Help the child finish his pie by stapling the crust to the top of the pie. Then invite each child to share his special pie with a classmate before he takes it home to share his yummy suggestion with his family.

Fine-Motor Fun

After teaching youngsters "There Was A Crooked Man," invite them to practice some crooked writing and cutting skills. Give each child a copy of page 39. Direct her to trace each line with a crayon; then have her cut along the crooked line. If desired, ask each child to reassemble her page and glue it onto a sheet of construction paper.

Shh! Timmy (child's name) is sleeping!

Shh! Gillian (child's name) is sleeping!

Do Not Disturb

Invite each child to create this special "Do Not Disturb" sign to follow up a recitation of "Wee Willie Winkie." Ask youngsters if they think that they could sleep with all the racket created by Wee Willie Winkie, then brainstorm ways in which the townspeople could let him know they are sleeping so they might not be disturbed. To make a sign, a child cuts out a tagboard copy of the sign pattern from page 40. Then he colors the sign, writes his name, and cuts out the doorknob hole. He adds foil stars to the nightcap as desired. Encourage each child to take his sign home to hang on his doorknob at bedtime. Shhh!

Mitten Match

Those three lovable kittens have once again lost their mittens! But your students can rescue them from their woes with this activity. After sharing this favorite rhyme with your class, give each child a copy of page 41. Instruct her to trace each line from the mitten on the left to its match on the right. After matching the mittens, have the child color each pair a different color. If desired, program the mitten pairs with color words. Meow! Meow!

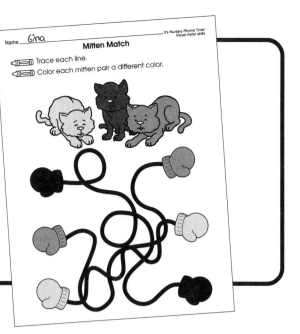

Mother Goose Goodies

Wee Willie Winkie's Warm Milk: Serve warm cocoa in Styrofoam® cups.

Mitten Munchies: Cut bread slices into mitten shapes with a cookie cutter. Brush melted butter over each; then sprinkle each with a sugar-cinnamon mixture. Toast the mittens until they are golden brown.

Crooked Man's Crooked Cookies: Pour melted butterscotch chips over small mounds of chow mein noodles. Serve cooled.

Dainty Dish Pies: For each pie, crumble a chocolate sandwich cookie into a mini pie shell. Top the pie with a dollop of whipped cream.

Character Day

Wrap up your Mother Goose unit with a special dress-up day to commemorate your students' many nursery rhyme favorites. For each child, duplicate a copy of the parent note on page 42. Ask each child to illustrate his favorite character on a notecard; then have him color and cut out his copy of the note. Help him cut along the bold line on the wing as shown. Then have him tape his illustration behind the wing so that it is visible when the wing is lifted. Send the notes home to parents. On the appointed day, lead youngsters on a character parade around the school.

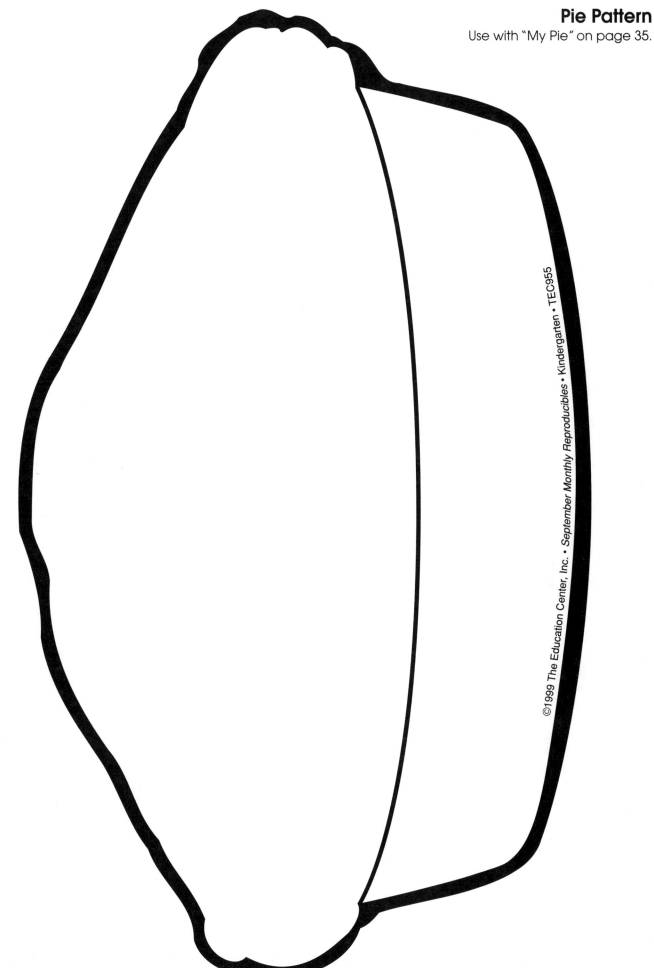

Piecrust Pattern

Use with "My Pie" on page 35.

Lift the crust to take a peek.
What do you see?
This is what I'd like to have
Baked in a pie for me!

©1999 The Education Center, Inc. • *September Monthly Reproducibles* • Kindergarten • TEC955

Name _____

It's Nursery Rhyme Time!
Writing/Cutting skills

Fine-Motor Fun

Trace.

Cut.

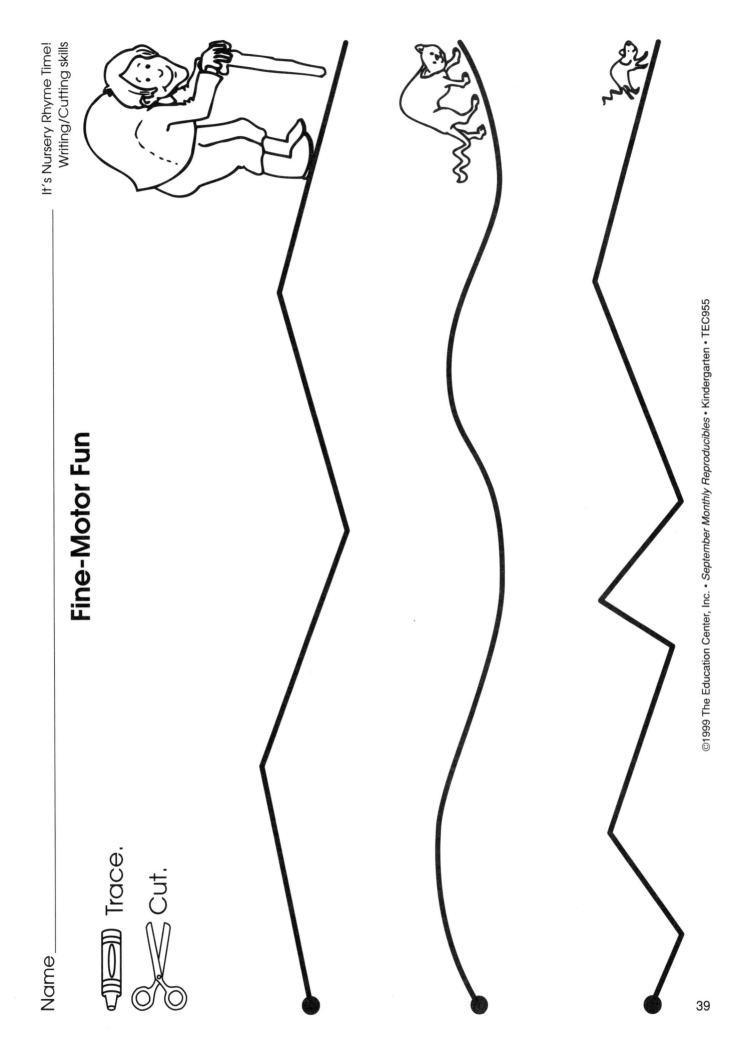

Doorknob Sign
Use with "Do Not Disturb" on page 35.

Name _____

It's Nursery Rhyme Time!
Visual-motor skills

Mitten Match

 Trace each line.

 Color each mitten pair a different color.

Dear Parent,

Our class will celebrate Character Day on _____. Please help
(date)
your child dress as his/her favorite nursery rhyme character on this day. (Look under Mother Goose's wing for a clue!) We look forward to seeing our Mother Goose favorites come to life!

Down On The Farm

Fetch your youngsters and come on down to the farm for a barn full of learning opportunities.

oops!

Oops, Wrong Family!

Challenge youngsters' visual-discrimination skills with this activity. Create several different arrangements of farm-animal counters (or small toys) so that there is one animal that doesn't belong in each group—for example, four ducks and one horse. Have student volunteers pick out the animals that don't belong. For independent practice, give each child a copy of page 45. Instruct him to circle the mismatched baby in each row, then color the page.

Chick And Piggy Puzzle

Here's a puzzle designed to reinforce your students' fine-motor and visual skills. Copy page 46 onto tagboard for each child. Invite her to color and cut apart her puzzle. Have the child place her puzzle pieces in a zippered plastic bag labeled with her name. Divide your class into student pairs and direct each student to assemble her partner's puzzle. After her partner checks the puzzle for correctness, have each student return the puzzle pieces to the bag. Then invite students to switch partners for another puzzling round of play.

Abbie

E-I-E-I-O! Lotto

This farm-animal matching game is sure to be a "lotto" fun! Duplicate pages 47 and 48 onto construction paper for each child; then make one extra copy of page 48. Color and cut out the extra set of animal cards (page 48) to use as caller cards. Have each child color and cut out his set of animal cards. Ask him to glue a different card onto each box of his gameboard. (He may keep the remaining three cards to use as he desires.) Appoint a volunteer to be the caller.

To play, the caller randomly selects an animal card. She then makes the sound for that animal. Each player with that animal on his card covers its picture with a counter. The first player (or players) to cover all the pictures on his card calls out "E-I-E-I-O!"

E-I-E-I-O!

chicken	sheep	cow
pig	horse	dog
goat	cat	duck

Read 'Til The Cows Come Home!

Extend your farm theme into students' homes with the handy bookmarks on page 49. Give each child a tagboard copy of one of the bookmarks to color, cut out, and take home. Encourage her to ask a family member to take her to the library or bookstore to find some of these "farm-tastic" stories!

In My Barnyard

Invite your little ones to use the reproducible on page 50 to create a fabulous farm scene. Duplicate the page for each child. Have him color the page, then cut out the pictures at the bottom. Encourage the child to arrange the pictures on the background as he chooses and glue them on the page. Then have him add to the scene by drawing any extra details he wants to include. During a group time, discuss the similarities and differences between two volunteers' pictures—being sure to note how two different pictures can *both* be wonderful!

Playing In The Hay

Give your students a supply of shredded-wheat cereal "hay bales" to practice a bundle of basic skills, such as the following:

- form letters and numerals with them *(pre-writing/ letter and numeral formation)*
- use them as manipulatives to solve story problems *(critical thinking)*
- use them as nonstandard forms of measurement *(math)*
- predict how many of them it takes to fill a container, then test the hypothesis *(science)*
- transfer them from bowl to bowl using a plastic fork as a pitchfork *(fine-motor)*
- crumble them to add texture to a piece of artwork *(art)*

44

Name_____

Oops, Wrong Family!

Circle the baby in each row that does not belong.

Color.

Puzzle

Use with "Chick And Piggy Puzzle" on page 43.

Animal Cards
Use with "E-I-E-I-O! Lotto" on page 43.

chicken

sheep

horse

goat

rooster

donkey

pig

cow

turkey

dog

duck

cat

Farmer Nat
Written by Chris Demarest
Published by Harcourt
Brace & Company

Parents In The Pigpen,
Pigs In The Tub
Written by Amy Ehrlich
Published by Puffin Books

No, No, Titus!
Written by Claire Masurel
Published by North-South
Books Inc.

Picnic Farm
Written by Christine Morton
Published by Holiday
House, Inc.

Waltz Of The Scarecrows
Written by
Constance W. McGeorge
Published by Chronicle Books

Cows In The Kitchen
Written by June Crebbin
Published by
Candlewick Press

Farmer Nat
Written by Chris Demarest
Published by Harcourt
Brace & Company

Parents In The Pigpen,
Pigs In The Tub
Written by Amy Ehrlich
Published by Puffin Books

No, No, Titus!
Written by Claire Masurel
Published by North-South
Books Inc.

Picnic Farm
Written by Christine Morton
Published by Holiday
House, Inc.

Waltz Of The Scarecrows
Written by
Constance W. McGeorge
Published by Chronicle Books

Cows In The Kitchen
Written by June Crebbin
Published by
Candlewick Press

©1999 The Education Center, Inc.

Name _____

50

In My Barnyard

Create a scene.

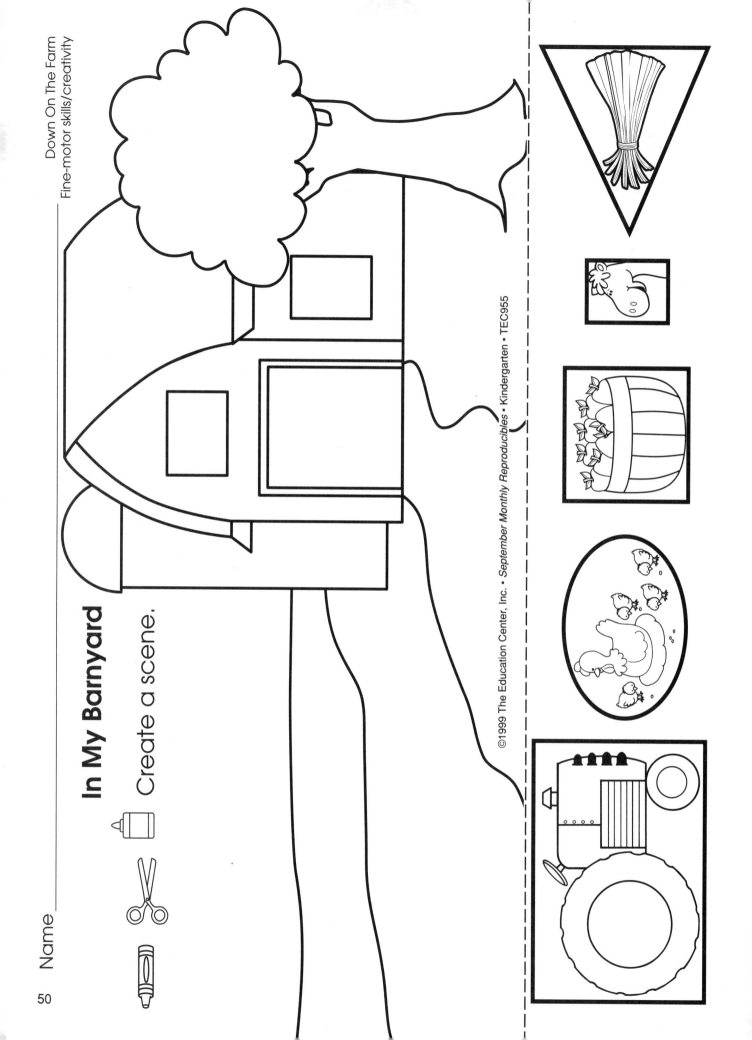

Thanks For Lunch!

The fourth week in September is set aside to recognize the contributions and importance of food service employees in our country. Here are some ideas to help honor these special workers in your own school.

Fancy Flowers

Students will be proud to present these fancy flowers to your school's food service workers. Prepare a set of templates by duplicating the flower patterns on page 52 onto three sheets of tagboard, then cutting out each flower size. To make a flower, trace each template on a piece of decorative gift wrap. Cut out the patterns and stack them from largest to smallest. Fold the stack in half; then punch a hole above the middle of the fold. Thread a pipe cleaner through the unfolded patterns to create a stem as shown. Gather the flower edges together and pinch the middle to give the bloom a more dimensional look. Invite each student to present her flower to a food service worker during a special ceremony (see "Appreciation Posters").

A Simple Serenade

Teach youngsters this sweet verse to sing to your food service workers. Although the words may be simple, they express the grandest of thoughts!

(sung to the tune of "Happy Birthday")

It's a special week for you.
It's a special week for you.
For all that you do,
We want to thank you!

Food Service Employees Are Special

Mrs. White always gives me a big scoop of potatoes.
Kristen

Mr. Clark always has a smile.
Joey

Mrs. White helps me count my change.
Lisa

Appreciation Posters

These posters will help youngsters communicate their appreciation for your school's food service employees. Divide your class into small groups; then work with one group at a time to make a poster. Title each poster "Food Service Employees Are Special." Then ask students to glue onto the poster magazine cutouts of foods they enjoy eating at school. Invite them to further embellish the poster with their own illustrations. Write each child's dictation about the food service workers on the poster. Then conduct a special ceremony to present the posters to this caring group of people, being sure to sing the song in "A Simple Serenade."

Flower Patterns

Use with "Fancy Flowers" on page 51.

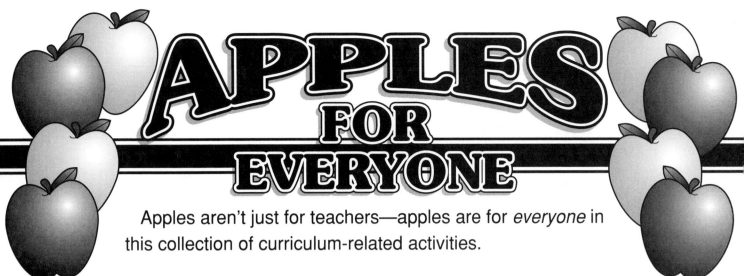

APPLES FOR EVERYONE

Apples aren't just for teachers—apples are for *everyone* in this collection of curriculum-related activities.

Apple Count

Count on this activity to reinforce youngsters' graphing and counting skills. In advance, bring in an assortment of red, green, and yellow apples. Put the apples in a basket in your math center. Also place a class supply of page 55 and a collection of red, green, and yellow crayons with the apples. Instruct each child in a small group to pick an apple from the basket and color a block on her paper that corresponds to the apple's color. Continue picking and coloring until the basket is empty. Then have youngsters count and compare the number of blocks colored in each column on their graphs.

Apple Math

Invite your students to create their own orchards with this idea. To begin, duplicate a class supply of page 56, and provide red, green, and yellow stamp pads. Instruct each child to color the trees, then to write a different numeral from 1 to 10 on the trunk of each tree. Have him use a different stamp-pad color to make the corresponding number of fingerprint apples on each tree.

Wormy Apples

These wormy apples are just right for wriggling some color-recognition skills out of your youngsters. To begin, duplicate a construction-paper worm pattern (page 57) for each color that is to be represented. Then duplicate a red construction-paper apple pattern (page 57) for each worm. Cut out all the patterns; then cut out the hole in each apple. Label each worm and apple set with the color name for the worm. Place the cutouts in a center. To use, a child inserts each worm into the apple labeled with the corresponding color name. There's not a bad apple in this bunch!

Apple Awards

Here's a tasty way to let little ones know that they are the apples of your eye! Duplicate and cut out a supply of the apple awards on page 58. Then, when you catch a student engaging in appropriate behavior or working diligently at a skill, fill out an award and present it to him. Periodically send each child home with an award *and* a fresh, delicious apple. Yummy!

A-Tisket, A-Tasket, An "Apple-bet" Basket

Learning the alphabet is a bushel of fun with this activity. To make a basket, duplicate, color, and cut out a tagboard copy of the pattern on page 59. Staple a zippered plastic bag to the back of the basket cutout. Duplicate the apple pattern on page 57 and mask the hole outline on the copy. Using this modified pattern, copy and cut out 26 construction-paper apples. Label each apple with a different letter; then put the apples in the plastic bag. To use, have a pair of students remove the cutouts from the bag, then sequence them using the alphabet printed on the basket as a guide.

For a future extension, randomly mask several letters on a copy of the basket pattern. Duplicate a class supply of the page; then challenge each youngster to fill in the missing letters.

Perfect Pickin's

Try this home-school connection to encourage parents to read to their children. Duplicate page 60 for each child to take home. Have parents write on each apple the title of a different book read at home. Then invite each child to color her page and bring it back to school. Display the completed pages along with the title "We've Read A Bushel Of Books!"

Name

Apple Count

Pick an apple from the basket.

What color is it?

Graph.

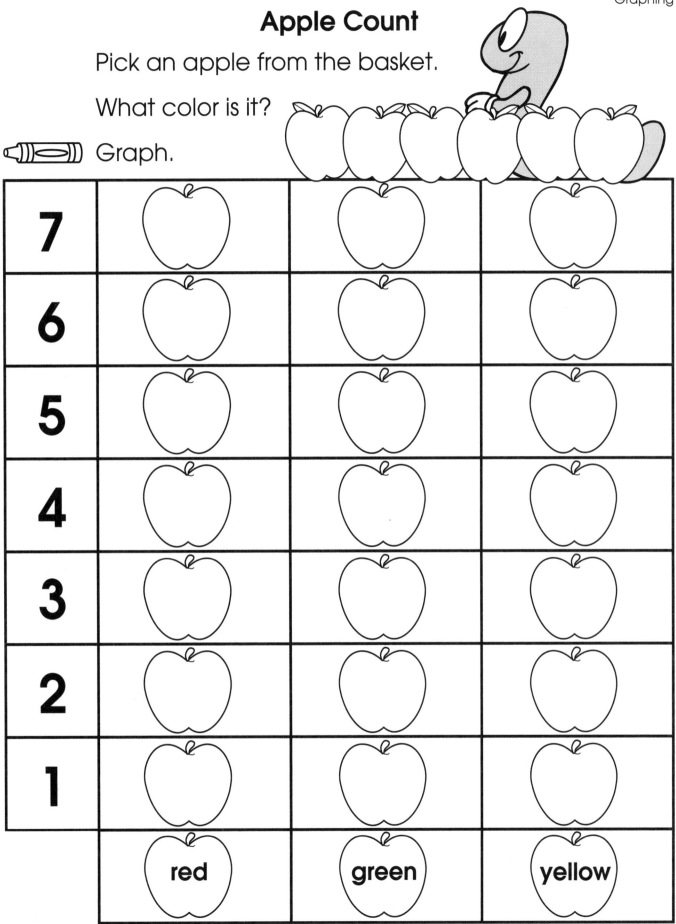

7			
6			
5			
4			
3			
2			
1			
	red	green	yellow

Names _____

56

Apple Math

🖍 Color the trees.

🖍 Write a different numeral on each tree.

👆 Make apples to match each numeral.

Patterns

Use both patterns with "Wormy Apples" on page 53.
Use the apple pattern with "A-Tisket, A-Tasket, An 'Apple-bet' Basket" on page 54.

Cut this out.

Awards

Use with "Apple Awards" on page 54.

_____ (Name)
is
GREAT

...all
the way to
the core!

_____ (Name)

took a
BITE

out of learning
today!

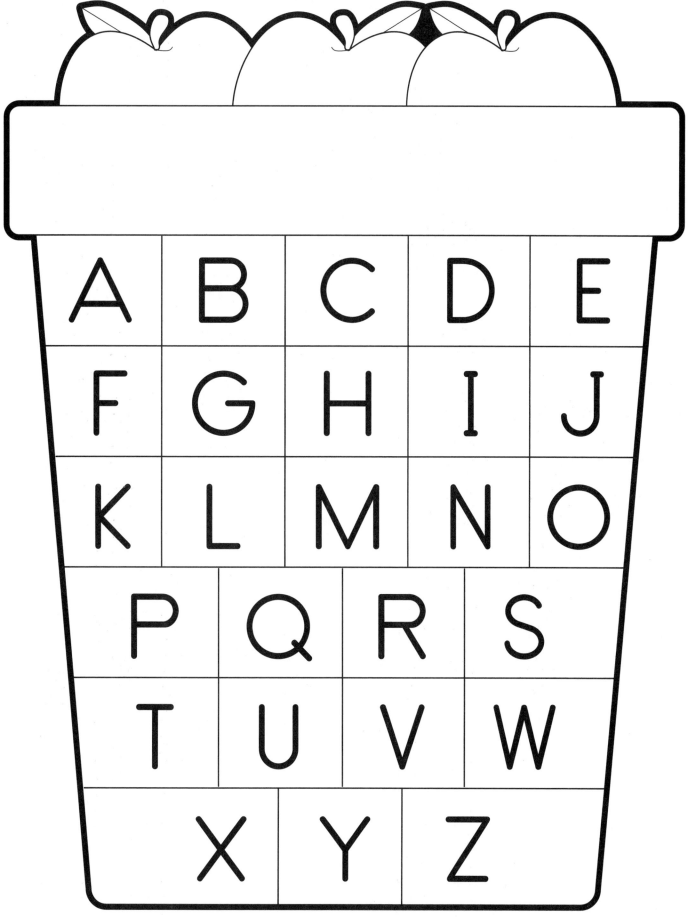

Dear Parent,
   Reading to your child is one of the best ways to promote literacy and develop an appreciation for books—not to mention the terrific quality time it provides. Please record (on the apples below) your child's favorite book "picks" from the reading you do together. Then have your child color the page and return it to school by
_____ to be displayed. Thank you!
   (Date)

Perfect Pickin's!

Reading Tree

National Dog Week

Hot diggety dog! The last full week of September is the time to celebrate National Dog Week—and these curriculum-related canine activities are perfect for the occasion!

In The Doghouse

Promote numeral recognition and counting skills with this simple activity. To begin, duplicate the patterns on page 62 onto construction paper. Color and cut out the doghouse, circles, and dogs. If desired, laminate the pieces for durability.

To use, a student places a circle cutout on the doghouse roof. Her partner then puts the corresponding number of dogs in the doghouse. Together, the students count the dogs to check for accuracy. Then the students switch roles and play again.

Big Dogs, Little Dogs

Use this idea to help youngsters bone up on their size-sequencing skills. For each child, duplicate the dog patterns on page 63. Have each child color and cut out her patterns. Then ask her to sequence the dogs by size—from largest to smallest or from smallest to largest—and glue them onto a sheet of construction paper.

Taking Care Of Man's Best Friend

These booklets will help youngsters understand some of the benefits and responsibilities of dog ownership. In advance, duplicate page 64 onto construction paper for each child. Discuss with your students the importance of caring for a dog properly. Invite students who own dogs to share their comments and experiences. Then give each child a copy of the booklet pages. Read aloud the cover and each page; then direct each child to color his booklet. Afterward, instruct each youngster to cut out his pages, sequence them behind the cover, and then staple the booklet together. Encourage students to take their booklets home to share with family members.

Patterns
Use with "In The Doghouse" on page 61.

How To Take Care Of A Dog

By _____

©1999 The Education Center, Inc.

Feed the dog. **1**

Brush the dog. **2**

Play with the dog. **3**